Mia Discovers

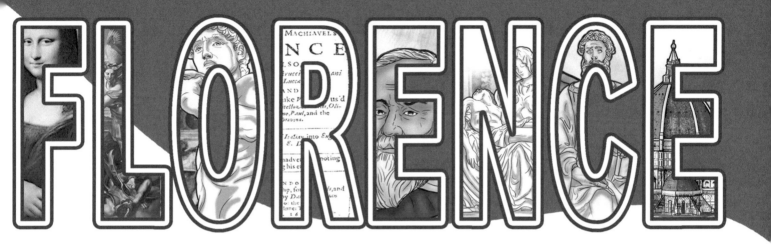

FLORENCE

by Alexandria Pereira

AuthorHouse™
1663 Liberty Drive
Bloomington, IN 47403
www.authorhouse.com
Phone: 833-262-8899

Because of the dynamic nature of the Internet, any web addresses or links contained in this book may have changed since publication and may no longer be valid. The views expressed in this work are solely those of the author and do not necessarily reflect the views of the publisher, and the publisher hereby disclaims any responsibility for them.

This book is printed on acid-free paper.

ISBN: 978-1-6655-4666-9 (sc)
ISBN: 978-1-6655-4665-2 (hc)
ISBN: 978-1-6655-4667-6 (e)

Library of Congress Control Number: 2021924856

Print information available on the last page.

Published by AuthorHouse 12/08/2021

authorHOUSE®

The Mystery of History Series
Book 4 of 4

Dedication

To my grandma - for her constant encouragement, wisdom and love.

"Good morning, Mia. Oh, what are you painting?" asked Grandma.

"Licorice, my new puppy! She looked so cute this morning sleeping, so I wantcd to paint her," said Mia.

"Mia, you are painting Licorice just like our ancestors' painted animals on cave walls," said Grandma.

"What are you talking about, Grandma?" asked Mia.

"Let me get a book and show you," said Grandma.

"Our Neanderthal ancestors liked to paint animals too. They painted animals on the walls of the places where they lived.

"You see, our Neanderthal ancestors so many centuries ago did not live in houses as we do today. They lived in caves. But just as we do today, they liked to paint. They painted on the walls of their caves, just as you are painting Licorice this morning.

"Do you know who else liked to paint and make a lot of art? The people of Florence in our Country of Italy," said Grandma.

"Could I see that art?" asked Mia.

"Why yes! Let's visit the museum today and learn about the history and art of Florence," said Grandma.

"Yes please," said Mia.

"The City of Florence was first started by the Etruscans. The Etruscans built a small town where Florence is today. Then many, many years later, the Romans came to that

small Etruscan town, and the town grew bigger. Then the Roman Empire came and gave Florence a government and rules to follow. The people worked hard and traded with each other. More and more people came, and Florence grew bigger and bigger.

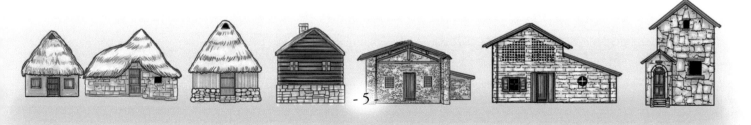

"Then many years later, the Roman Empire ended, and so did its government and rules. Now the people started to fight, and armies came and tried to take things the people had. So, the people decided to find a new way to protect themselves. They built big stone walls around their city to keep the armies out and the people inside safe. The people made their own rules, and made their own government. This helped the people work better together.

"Now the people of Florence felt safe behind the big stone walls. Florence became a very powerful city. The people could work on new things and have new ideas. The people in Florence could now trade more easily. They traded wool for spices, silks, and other fine things. Those things then were traded again with other people in other cities, and the traders made a lot of money.

One trader, Giovanni de' Medici, used the money he made from trading to start a bank. This bank made a lot more money for Giovanni. He, his son Cosimo, and his grandson Lorenzo used this money to pay artists to make beautiful art. They also paid scientists to discover new ideas about math and science, engineers to build amazing buildings, and writers to write wonderful stories.

"These artists, scientists, engineers, and writers discovered their great ideas by reading old books, looking at old drawings, and studying old buildings. They learned from one another and asked a lot of questions. They learned how art, science, engineering, and writing were done centuries before by their ancestors, the Greek and early Roman people. They then used what they learned to discover new things, have new ideas, and make art, science, engineering, and writing in new ways.

"One amazing artist was Leonardo di Vinci. He painted paintings and sculpted statues for homes and churches. He also designed machines and musical instruments. Some of these designs we still use today.

Another amazing artist was Michelangelo. He was a painter and sculptor, as well as an engineer and writer. He painted the ceiling of the Sistine Chapel. He sculpted a giant statue of a man, named David, and a smaller statue of a mother and her child. He also wrote some poetry, just because he learned how to.

"Then there was Raphael. He painted amazing paintings for homes and churches.

Donatello, who sculpted many different kinds of statues, used what he learned to show people his ideas.

And of course, Lorenzo Ghiberti, who made some famous bronze doors, sculpted statues in bronze using what he learned.

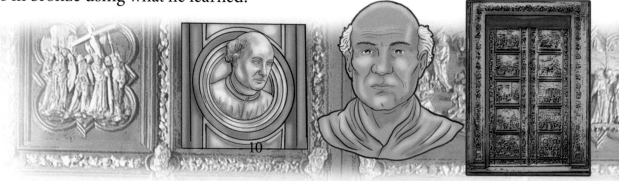

"Galileo Galilei was an astronomer, physicist, and engineer. Galileo discovered a lot about the sky and planets. He made new discoveries about how things work. And he invented a way to test ideas about science—the scientific method that we still use today.

The engineer Filippo Brunelleschi was an architect, designer, and sculptor. He designed and managed the construction of Florence Cathedral and its famous dome, known as the Duomo. He also designed machines that would make building easier.

The writer and poet Niccolò Machiavelli was a diplomat, philosopher, and writer. He wrote books that kings, presidents, and military leaders would read and use many years later.

"All the things they learned, all the new ideas they had, and all the great art, science, engineering, and writing that was made in Florence spread to other cities such as Venice and Rome. Then it spread all over the Country of Italy and even to other countries. As trading increased, more and more money was made. Rich traders, kings and queens asked these artists, scientists, engineers, and writers to visit their cities and make new things for them.

"Even though a few more armies came to take control of Florence, in the end, the art, science, engineering, and writing continued. The people continued to work together, make rules together, and find new ways to learn and have new ideas. They helped Florence and the whole Country of Italy grow. They did this, and now you, Mia, can be here today and decide to paint Licorice using what you have learned. Thank you for using paper and not the walls of our house to paint on," said Grandma.

"Heh heh, Grandma, of course," Mia said.

"A lot has happened in Florence Italy since my ancestors first lived," Mia said. "I can see all the changes my family has made over so many, many years so that I could be here today. I now can learn new things, have new ideas, and make art, science, engineering, and writing in my own way. This was my and Florence's history. Thank you, Grandma," said Mia.

"You are very welcome, Mia," said Grandma.

Florence Timeline

800 BC	Etruscans start a small settlement on the banks of the Arno River near where the City of Florence is today.
59	Florence begins to grow when Romans arrive and populate the town.
541 AD	The first of the city walls is constructed. Walls continue to be added as the town grows in the ninth, eleventh, twelfth, and thirteenth centuries.
570	The Lombard army makes its way through Tuscany.
1115	Florence forms the first *commune*, or city-state, and is run by an assembly of one hundred citizens.
1235	The florin is first minted in silver and then in 1252 in gold. The florin is used as a standard coin in Europe though the 1500s.
1250	Trade guilds gain power.
1296	Construction for the Duomo begins.
1434	The Medici family starts their rise to power in Florence.
1469	Niccolò Machiavelli born in Florence.
1492	Italian Renaissance reaches its high point.
1503	Leonardo da Vinci paints the *Mona Lisa*.
1508	Michelangelo begins painting the ceiling of the Sistine Chapel.
1570	The Tuscan state is formed, free from the Holy Roman Empire.
1797	Napoleon's army invades Italy.
1865	Florence is made the capital of the newly formed Kingdom of Italy.
1946	The Italian Republic is formed. Women gain the right to vote.
1999	Italy joins the European Union as one of six founding members.

Education Support Activities

Basic Human Needs

food
shelter
clothing
the need to socialize
the need to solve problems, invent, and be
creative

Practical Life and Sensorial Foundation

engage children in activities characteristic of
Italy
plant a seed
wash grapes
paint a picture

History

past, present, and future
timelines

Science

sculpt a clay figure
make a model of a city wall

Geography and Map Work

continents
Europe
significant landforms

Botany

focus on grapes and olive oil, and other
agricultural products of Italy

Earth Science

volcanoes

Peace Curriculum

peace table process
conflict resolution skills

Printed in the United States
by Baker & Taylor Publisher Services